Africa's Big Three

Written and photographed by Jonathan and Angela Scott

Contents

Collins

Africa's big three

The huge African savannah is made up of grassland and some woodland. It's home to three of the largest animals on Earth: elephants, rhinos and hippos.

Elephants are the biggest.

Hippos are smaller than elephants and live on the banks of rivers and lakes.

Rhinos are also smaller than elephants but they can be as big as trucks.

3

Elephants

Elephants are very peaceful animals, but they need a lot of food and water. They eat grass and leaves all day and during the night as well.

Did you know?

An elephant can eat over 200 kilograms of food a day. It can drink up to 225 litres of water a day.

An elephant's tusks are teeth which grow throughout the elephant's life. They are made of ivory.

An elephant's trunk has 15,000 muscles! It's strong enough to pull down a young tree, but it can also pick up a small fruit.

tusks

trunk

skin

Elephant skin is very tough.

Elephants live in groups called herds.
Male elephants are called bulls and
females are called cows.

Full-grown elephants don't have many enemies
as they are too big and strong.

However a lion or hyena may sometimes attack
a young or sick elephant.

Elephants live for 60 to 70 years and the cows stay with their family group all their lives.

Baby elephants are called calves and need their mothers to look after them, but all the elephants in the group help to bring up the young ones.

Male elephants leave the group when they are between 10 and 15 years old. Then they wander, often with other males, looking for new groups.

Rhinos (or rhinoceroses)

African rhinos have two horns on their heads. These are made of the same kind of material as our fingernails.

Rhinos have bad eyesight and they look clumsy. But few animals would dare to attack them. They have excellent hearing and they can be bad-tempered.

A rhino can run faster than a human.
It can also dodge and turn very quickly.

There are two kinds of African rhino:
the "white" rhino and the black rhino.

Both kinds live alone or in very small groups.
They are fully grown at five to seven years old.
They can live for up to 40 years.

Did you know?

The white rhino isn't white at all. It has a wide upper lip, so the word "white" should really be "wide".

Black rhino

White rhino

pointed upper lip

wide upper lip

12

Rhinos usually have one baby, called a calf. Rhino mothers look after their calves for several years.

13

Hippos (or hippopotamuses)

The name "hippopotamus" means "river horse".

Hippos like to spend most of the day in the water. They breathe air but they can walk underwater on the river bed for several minutes.

A hippo's skin must stay moist and it can get sunburnt out of the water.

Hippos come out of the water at night. Then they eat grass, just like cows.

Hippos can run fast, just like rhinos, and they will attack if they are in danger. A hippo feels safest in the water.

16

A hippo can open its mouth wider than any other mammal, and it has huge teeth called tusks. A hippo can bite a small boat in half.

Hippos live in groups of between 10 and 20 females with their babies, guarded by a powerful male, called a bull.

18

Mother hippos have one baby, called a calf, and they look after it until it is about five to eight years old. Hippos can live for up to 35 years.

People and the big three

People are the worst enemies of elephants, rhinos and hippos.

The savannah where the big three live is shrinking. People farm the land and build their homes on it.

People kill elephants for their ivory tusks. They kill hippos for meat and oil, and rhinos for their horns. Today, black rhinos are very rare.

These elephant tusks are being burned to stop people from selling them.

Game wardens try to stop the hunters but many animals are still killed. We need to protect Africa's big three animals, before they are all gone.

Factfile: Africa's big three

	African elephant	White rhino
How long do they live?	60-70 years	30-40 years
How rare are they?	becoming rare	rare
Fantastic fact	has 15,000 muscles in its trunk	has a wide lip

Black rhino	Hippo
30-40 years	up to 35 years
very rare	becoming rare
has a pointed lip	can bite a small boat in half

Ideas for reading

Written by Linda Pagett B.Ed(hons), M.Ed
Lecturer and Educational Consultant

Learning objectives: scan texts to find specific sections; pose questions prior to reading; evaluate a text for its purpose; use synonyms; work effectively in groups, ensuring each group member takes a turn, challenging, supporting and moving on

Curriculum links: Geography: Passport to the world; Citizenship: Animals and us; Science: Plants and animals

Interest words: elephants, rhinoceroses, hippopotamuses, savannah, grassland, woodland

Word count: 778

Resources: small whiteboard and pens

Getting started

This book may be read over two sessions.

- Show the children the book and ask them to read the title. Ask them what the *Big Three* are. Read the blurb together and ask them if they can answer any of the questions.

- Ask the children what features they would expect to see inside a non-fiction book (*headings, labels, photographs*).

- Discuss what they want to find out about the big three, and write the questions on the whiteboard.

- Using the contents page, give the children certain sections to read and explain that they will feed back information to the rest of the group.

Reading and responding

- While the children are reading, remind them to pay attention to details in photos and use phonological and contextual knowledge to work out unfamiliar words such as *savannah*.

- Ask the children in pairs to practise answering the questions on the whiteboard. If they don't know the answers, encourage them to go back and reread their section.

- Children report back to the group on what they have found out.